Facebook Marketing

Growing Your Facebook Audience And Turning Them Into Profitable Customers For Your Business Through Selling And Affiliate Marketing

Brad Tiller

Table of Contents

Introduction

Congratulations on downloading *"Facebook Marketing!"*

This marketing guide is up-to-date on all of the most recent and relevant information regarding Facebook marketing. Everything you will learn within will support you in understanding how you can maximize your sales and income through your Facebook business page, beginning with creating and optimizing your page.

Facebook is one of the most lucrative online marketing platforms available. Despite originating as a social sharing site used primarily amongst family and close friends, Facebook has quickly expanded to include a wonderful opportunity for businesses to share and promote to their target audience directly through a platform that they check into approximately 8 times per day.

Taking advantage of this platform will assist you in reaching a large portion of your audience that you may not already be tapped into. If you are already using Facebook, this guide will support you in learning how to optimize your usage to get the best engagement and return on your time investment.

Facebook marketing is an essential tool for any business that wants to succeed in the 21st century. With everything going online, having your business "plugged in" and directly in front of your audience is essential. Not only will it support you in accessing them and staying relevant, but it will also help you in increasing your business, allowing you to tap into a global network of users that range in demographics.

After more than thirteen years in business, Facebook knows what it is doing and knows how to optimize its platform for the user experience. This includes connecting businesses and ideal customers so that you can reap in more sales while your customers gain access to the products they want and need.

If you are ready to begin maximizing your online exposure, increasing your sales, and reaching a larger capacity of your target audience, you have come to the right place! Take advantage of this incredible marketing tool now by applying the tools you use in this book! And of course, enjoy!

Chapter 1: The Value of Facebook

Facebook is an incredibly powerful marketing tool that is essential for any successful 21st-century business owner to take advantage of. Businesses that are not actively using Facebook in some way, shape, or form are robbing themselves of massive profit increase potential. It continues to be one of the leading social networking platforms, making it a huge tool for accessing your target market and increasing your sales.

Here are some of the reasons why you need to be taking advantage of Facebook for marketing your business:

Massive Number of Active Users

The sheer size of Facebook's active users alone should be enough to encourage any company to lay down roots on the Facebook network. Facebook has more than 1 billion active users visiting its site on a daily basis, and more than 2 billion active monthly visitors. This means that on a daily basis, you are tapping into a market that accounts for 1/7ths to 2/7ths of the entire global population. The reach is so massive making it a highly valuable tool for marketers to use.

Evenly Split Demographics

Every network has it's demographic audience, but almost none stack up to Facebook. Facebook is unique in a sense that it has a very evenly split demographic. Its users are a strong balance of

men and women from nations all across the globe. With this balance, it is almost a given that your niche will be hanging out on Facebook, ready to consume your content!

Global Network

Facebook has a strong North American presence, but it actually has an incredibly strong international presence as well. India, Brazil, and Indonesia account for a great deal of the active daily audience after the US. This means that you can expand your target audience far beyond the core and capitalize in a far bigger way using Facebook.

Language Translation

Something that regularly holds people back from being able to conduct business across borders is language barriers. Not being able to communicate with international audience in a language they understand can ultimately hinder your ability to sell overseas. Not anymore, though! Facebook has more than 70 translations available on its platform, meaning that users from all around the world can read your page and purchase anything you may be selling. The fact that the feature is built-in makes it far more accessible and user-friendly, maximizing the potential for international users to hang out and read what you have been sharing about! Instead of your business being nation wide it can easily target the whole world.

60% of Users Like Pages

On Facebook, only 40% of users have never liked a page before. 60% of them have liked pages, with the majority of them liking multiple pages. Right now, more than 60 million businesses have Facebook pages that are capitalizing on Facebook's marketplace. What is also worth noting is that 39% of users, who have liked a page, like the pages specifically for the purpose of receiving a special offer from that page. This means that your followers are more than likely looking to purchase and are staying plugged into your Facebook page to see the latest and greatest deals you are offering!

Frequent Tune-In Rates

Facebook is one of the most returned-to social networking sites to presently exist. Users spend an average of 35 minutes per day on the application every check-in and a user usually check-in almost over 8 times. This means that they are coming back to see what is going on. If you are taking advantage of the platform, you may just be a part of the feed that they are checking in on all day long!

Inexpensive Cost per Click Advertising

From a business standpoint, having an affordable cost-per-click advertising feature is extremely important. This means that if (and when) you choose to use paid advertising features; you are going to be paying an extremely affordable rate for your advertisements. The average cost-per-click fee on Facebook as of 2018 is $1.72. This can be greatly reduced with proper metrics as well. This means that you may end up paying even less for the same great value!

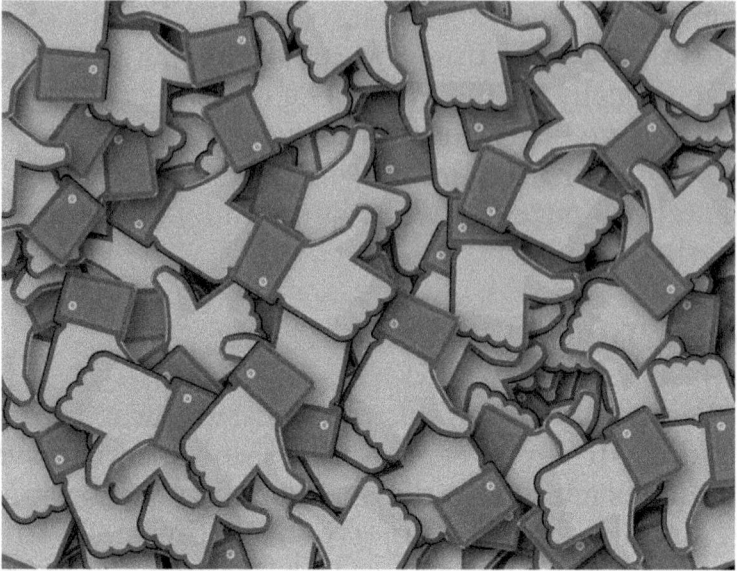

Chapter 2: Optimizing Your Page

If you want to get the most out of Facebook, you need to start with a page that is optimized to win. It is important that you are intentional about how you create this part of your platform because certain aspects of your Facebook page cannot be changed once they are fixed in place. For example, the name of your page can be slightly altered but cannot be changed completely. For that reason, you need to make sure that you choose the right name the first time.

You also need to know which aspects of your page you need to pay attention to and customize. The more customized your page is, the more knowledge and information your audience can gain just through scrolling your page. This is important because it can be the difference between someone being interested and finding what they need, or someone losing interest because there is not enough information available to them.

Here is what you need to do to create and optimize your Facebook page for maximum impact.

Create Your Business Name and User Name

Creating your Facebook page requires you to start by creating a business name. If you already have a business, use the name you are currently using for that. If not, take a few minutes to consider what name you want to use. It is important that you use a name that will be easy to remember, spell, and identify. If you are already active on other social sharing sites, make sure you use the same name so that people can easily find you on any platform.

When you are creating the actual business name for your page, you can use spaces. You should refrain from using any punctuation whatsoever because this will look unprofessional. The business name for your page is also the title of your page, which does not require anything like periods. If you have natural punctuation included, such as "Reid's Candy Shop" you can use this. However, refrain from turning your title into a short sentence.

In addition to creating a business name for your page, you are also given the opportunity to create a username for your page. This is a simple username that can be searched in the Facebook search bar so that your followers can find you. If you have other social networking platforms, this should be *exactly* the same username as you are using elsewhere. This makes it easier for you to be found. If you do not, create one that can be used across all platforms as this will make it easy to branch out. Again, make it sweet and simple, to the point, easy to spell, and free of any punctuation. In this case, even the apostrophe should be ignored in favor of simplicity.

Customize Your Information

Now that your basic page is created, it is time to go in and customize all of the information on your page. The easiest way to do this is on a desktop because it allows easier access to all of the customizable features. From the desktop, access your page and then navigate to the "About" tab. Here, you will see the option to edit your page's information. You want to go into the settings and customize virtually everything. Identify exactly what "theme" your page is (artist, coach, entrepreneur, etc.). You should also fill in a small description about your page, the short bio that people see when they search for you, and your businesses story if you have one. You should also update your contact information so that you can easily be reached or accessed, especially if you have a storefront, people will know where to find you.

Customizing all of this information is necessary if you want to have a strong business page that will serve your clients in a way that supports them in shopping with you. Your audience wants to know everything they can before purchasing. Making it all available in one simple spot makes it extremely easy for them to identify anything they need to know.

Design Your Page

Now that the information contained within your page is completed, you need to go ahead and design your page. Your page should look uniformed and attractive. This means that you should have a set theme and color scheme that you are using, and everything should be done in a way that features high-quality images so that people are instantly drawn in and curious to learn more about your business.

Upon creating your page, Facebook will allow you to upload a profile photo and cover photo. You want to pick photographs that accurately represent your business and align with the image you are creating. You will learn more about this in *"Chapter 3: Your Image."*

Chapter 3: Your Image

It is likely that you have uploaded some basic imagery for your page upon creating your site. Now, it is time to really nail down your "look" and master it. When you are building or expanding your online presence, it is essential that you get it properly. Having a poor quality image that does not look visually appealing and can greatly inhibit your success because it prevents people from wanting to look at your content. Remember, social media has been around for a while now which has allowed marketers to set the bar pretty high. While it certainly runs by achievable high standards, you do have to do more than simply throwing up a basic image and calling it a day. Everything needs to look a specific way to attract your audience and encourage them to follow and engage with your site.

Here is what you need to do to create a custom image that attracts your target audience.

Find Your Edge

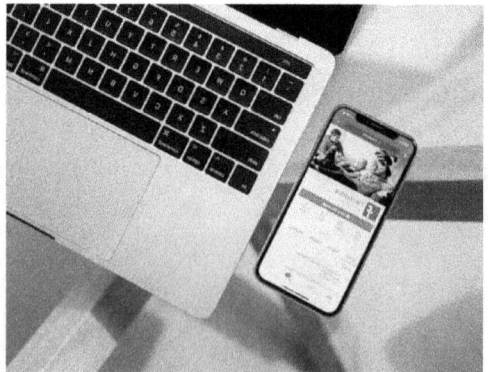

Before you really dig into creating your image, it is a good idea to find your edge. This requires you to take a look at your competition and see what they are doing on Facebook. Take some time to identify what their theme is, what color scheme they are using, and how it is helping them interact with your shared audience. You may begin to notice a trend of what color schemes and themes seem to work best with your audience. When you do notice this trend, use it to help you identify your own way of fitting into the marketplace.

The key to finding your edge is knowing what everyone else is doing and then doing it better. You want to see what is helping others succeed and then customize your own theme and color scheme that looks and performs better than anyone else's. When you do this, you begin to create a unique look that supports you in having a greater impact on reaching your target audience. When they see why you are different and better, they are more interested in following you.

Get A Logo and Cover Art Made

Facebook allows you to have a profile picture and cover art. While you can easily throw up any image, having branded images looks infinitely better. You can make this yourself, but it is recommended that you leave it to a graphic designer. Having an image that is attractive and that accurately represents your business is important. Facebook's sizing differences between mobile and desktop can sometimes make images blurry, so having a professional create your images can save you a headache and give you the opportunity to have great imagery that looks high quality as well. Remember, blurry, pixelated, or otherwise low-quality photographs will not suffice in online marketing in the 21st century.

Great places to hire professional graphic designers for a reasonable fee include Upwork, Fiverr, and 99 designs. Websites like Upwork and Fiverr will typically only charge around $5-$10 per image which makes them incredibly affordable. 99 designs do cost quite a bit more, but they also give you many options to choose from and tend to have higher quality imagery. You should choose the one that best fits your budget and needs.

Creating an Attractive Profile

Creating an attractive profile requires two things: static content that is consistent and high quality, and posts that are consistent and high quality. You want to maintain the same color palette and theme throughout your whole page. While not every single picture you post may be rooted in your color scheme, it should make sense to your overall theme and look attractive on the page that you are creating.

Pay attention to how you are posting, what you are posting, and how it all fits with what you are sharing overall. If anything does not make sense or does not amplify or enhance the overall aesthetic, theme, and message of your page, then you should refrain from posting it. Staying higher quality and trendy is important because it ensures that people enjoy scrolling your page and are more likely to follow you and revisit your page on a regular basis.

Where to Find Images for Posting

Finding images to post on your page can sometimes be challenging. However, it does not have to be. There are a few things that you need to know, however. The first thing is that you should be seeking images that are free of copyright. Royalty-free stock images are a great place to start because they provide you with great, high-quality images that you do not have to credit anyone for when you are using them. Plus, you do not have to worry about copyright infringement! Websites like Pixabay or Unsplash are great ones to go to for searching what images you want to use on your page. You can easily save the images and share them on your page with whatever caption and content you desire. Additionally, you can easily search for images that suit your theme and color scheme, so that they stay on-brand and keep your page looking beautiful and attractive to your audience.

A Word about Copyright

It is extremely important that you are cautious about copyright laws and refrain from using any image that features some form of copyright on it. If you find an image and are unsure about the copyright law behind it, refrain from using it. Using images with copyright can lead to lawsuits that are costly and that ultimately damage your business's reputation and your bottom line. It is much safer and easier to refrain from using them at all and keeping yourself protected and professional. Any image marketed as "royalty free" means that the image does not have any copyright law attached to it that requires you to credit or pay the artist. This means that you will not have to worry about copyright infringement and you can use the image as you please. There are hundreds of thousands of stock images online, so you can easily find new ones without having to reuse old ones. Plus, more are regularly being updated to popular sites like the aforementioned ones, Pixabay and Unsplash, on a daily basis!

Chapter 4: Reaching Your Audience

The entire purpose of marketing is that you want to reach your target audience. With Facebook being so massive and featuring an international span of users, you can guarantee that you have the ability to reach your target audience on this platform. The important thing is to know *how* to reach your target audience quickly and efficiently so that you do not waste any time attempting to market to people who are completely irrelevant to your niche. This can take some practice, but we are going to give you the steps you need to make it extremely simple to learn how.

Research Your Audience

The first step to reaching your audience is to know who they are. After all, you cannot talk to someone you do not know! With the many different uses for Facebook, you have a great opportunity to take some time to identify who your target audience is and learn more about what they are doing. The best way to start reaching your target audience is to go ahead and follow the pages of your competitors and begin paying attention to who follows *them*. Start with the ones who follow your competitors and actively engage with their posts. However, you can also peek through their "followers" list and get an idea of who the demographic is.

When you are researching your audience, be as specific as you can. Identify what gender they tend to be, what age they are, where they live, whether or not they have families, and what they do in their spare time. The more you know about your audience, the easier it is to target them. When it comes to Facebook, you especially want to pay attention to being thorough. This is because later on when you begin to move into paid advertising, you can have the option to be very specific about whom you want to advertise to. Knowing this information already will make it easier to reach your audience organically as well as to maximize your reach through paid advertising. Then, when they land on your page, you have a clear idea of who they are, what they care about, and what they are looking for. That means your entire page should be geared toward them, making them more likely to enjoy what they see and stick around to follow you and engage with your posts.

Your competitors can give you great insight and inspiration to reach your audience, but reaching your audience is the end goal. When you spend time on social sharing networks such as Facebook, you get a competitive edge because you are able to see your audience living their daily lives. You can follow them and engage with them online, which not only increases your brand awareness but also gives you the opportunity to understand what your audience cares about and what they are interested in. When you get to know your audience in this more intimate way, it becomes easier to understand what you should post to gain their awareness and attention.

Look around on the Internet at different blogs, forums, and other social sharing networks to see what they are doing and what draws their attention. This gives you a greater understanding of their mannerisms and interests, allowing you to post with greater ease and confidence because you know exactly what they are interested in. Staying on top of finding problems that your audience are having related to your niche and then solving that for them is what will differentiate you from your competition.

Business is about solving problems, so always make sure you intend to do that in the most professional and creative way possible.

Finding problems within your niche is easy to find by looking through the comments on social media pages and asking questions, showing your interest towards your audience. I've also found that researching your customers on Forums works best. For example: On Google, just simply type in (The keyword from your niche) forums – Advice needed. Doing this will come up with a load of forums of people discussing their own thoughts towards the topic, making it much easier for you to target your audience on Social media, which will then ultimately make them more intrigued towards your Facebook Page if you're answering and solving the problems they have. You can do this through posting certain quotes, certain facts and by captioning your photo to get your followers to comment and discuss their thoughts.

Hang Out Where Your Audience Hangs Out

Spending time in places such as social media pages and forums, especially when your business is smaller, gives you the opportunity to connect one to one with your audience. It becomes easier to build relationships with potential followers and then direct them to your page so that they can support you and your business.

This may sound time-consuming, but it does not have to take more than a few minutes per day. Logging on and spending even just ten to fifteen minutes frequenting popular hangout spots and commenting and engaging with followers will make you known and increase your visibility. As a result, your brand awareness will increase as well, and you will maximize your follower potential. Plus, since you have already established relationships with these people, their followers will generally be more engaged and sincere.

This means that they will likely be an active follower and a 'warm-to-hot' lead for your business.

Remember to like every popular Facebook page and follow your niche on all social media platforms. You want to be obsessed with you niche so you can create ideas through what has worked from your competitors.

Find Followers on Other Sites

Many Facebook users like to use other sites as a way to drive additional traffic to their page. This can be more complex, such as hanging out in popular forums as we have already discussed. Or, it can be extremely simple. For example, if you already have a presence built on your website or on another social media site, such as Instagram, you can link your Facebook page over to these pages. This means that anyone who currently follows you there can see that you are on Facebook and click over to follow you. This is a very easy and yet highly effective way of showing people where you are online, so be sure to take advantage of it.

Targeting the Right Audience

This may sound obvious, but targeting the right audience is necessary. Due to Facebook's algorithms and design, there are literally thousands of niches that are presently on Facebook. Knowing exactly what niche is yours and then using that information to learn how to target them appropriately is essential. You do not want to waste any of your time marketing toward the wrong people.

It may sound daunting to have to know minute details about your audience, but the reality is that it is actually ingenious. While it may take a little bit of research and trial and error to get there, once you know exactly who your target audience is, it becomes insanely easy to target them and have them find you. Make sure that everything you do is targeting your audience effectively. Use the right colors, images, and vocabulary to encourage them to find your page interesting and want to stay around to see what you have to offer.

Optimizing Competitor's Ideas

A great way to maximize your following is to capitalize on what your competitors are doing. For example, if your competitors are all partaking in a certain trend and doing it one way, see if you can customize it and do it on your own unique way in a manner that still keeps you relevant but also sets you apart. This is called creating your edge. Creating your edge allows you to fit into your industry perfectly, but in a way that sets you apart from others in your industry.

A great reason why you want to optimize on your competitors' ideas is that you can already see the stats (likes and comments) on what they have done. You can clearly tell if it is working or not, and often, you can see exactly what could have been done better to make it more effective. Having access to this type of information without having to learn it firsthand can be invaluable because it means you have the potential to do far better and thus, have return results that are way more impressive than your competitors.

Chapter 5: Drawing Traffic To Your Facebook Page

Getting Reviews

Facebook reviews are like Facebook currency. When you have great reviews on your page, you tend to be far more visible to your target audience. You are also given a unique ability to show your audience that you are performing well and that they can trust in you and your products or services. Most people are under the impression that the only time someone speaks up is when there is a problem. So, seeing a page that has tons of great reviews means that your product or service is so great that it actually inspired people to talk about it and share that with you.

Getting reviews is actually incredibly easy. The best way to do it is to follow up after a service or product has been sold to a person and they have received it. Give them some time and then follow up by asking them if they are happy with their purchase. If they are, kindly ask if they would share a review so that others can see how incredible it was. Most individuals who have enjoyed their product or service are more than happy to share a review. Plus, since you are following up, anyone who feels that the product or service was not satisfying can easily let you know what was wrong and you can take care of it. This is a great way of building customer relationships and rapport while also receiving reviews that will support you in acquiring future sales.

Requesting Engagement

One great way to get engagement on your posts is to ask for it. With Facebook, it is as easy as sharing a relatable image or quote and saying "Can you relate?" or "Share this with a friend who gets it!" Subtle yet direct requests like this encourage people to share your posts with others, increasing your engagement. As with most social media platforms, when your engagement goes up, the number of people who see your posts go up as well. Getting regular engagement and increasing the amount of engagement you get is important. This will make you easier to find, more visible, and more likely to get sales.

Giveaways

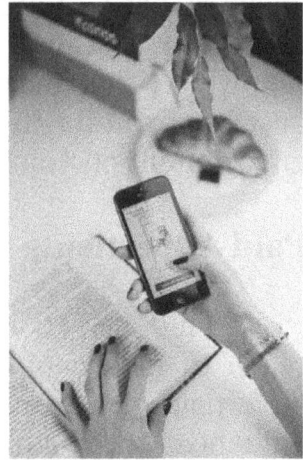

Giveaways are always a great way to maximize engagement and increase your followers. You can do giveaways on Facebook easily with just a little bit of planning. Start by choosing what product or service you want to give away. Make sure it is something that will be attractive and desirable to your audience but won't cost you too much to give away for free. You want a healthy ratio of engagement and new followers to earn money invested through the free product. This makes it worthwhile. Giving away something too expensive or valuable in exchange for fewer followers is not a good tradeoff, so refrain from doing this. Once your page is much larger, you can consider doing bigger giveaways. But in the meantime, refrain from this and stick to more reasonable ones that will still appeal to your audience in a big way.

After you have chosen the item or service you want to give away, you can make your post. Be sure to set your end date, so people know when to check back by. Ideally, this should be two to three weeks in the future. Then, go ahead and make your post. There are three things you need to include in this post. These things should be presented as the rules that are required to enter the giveaway. They include: asking for them to like your page, asking for them to like your post, and asking for them to tag a friend/s. Many companies will also include a rule that allows the contestants to share the post to their page (as a public post) for an additional entry into the draw. Including these rules ensures that you are going to actually receive engagement from your post in a way that shares it beyond your current following. This maximizes your reach and gives you the best opportunity to gain new followers and increase your engagement on your page overall.

Paid Advertising

Paid advertising can be a great way to increase your reach to new people. On Facebook, the metrics for paid advertising are very specific. This is where knowing your audience well can pay off. When you create your promotions, you can set an end date, choose your budget, and then target your audience. Through your custom target options, you can make extremely specific metrics that ensure that only those who are actually likely to purchase from you will see the ad. This ensures that you are not wasting any of your budgets on people who will not purchase from you.

Facebook allows you to host ads in many ways, including boosting posts that you have already made, creating and promoting new posts, and doing an ongoing promotion for your page. You can also choose what your goal is, such as getting new followers, increasing engagement, getting messages, or making sales by driving people to your website. Using these features, you can customize the perfect advertisement that will maximize your reach and get you a great result from your advertisement.

Setting up ad campaigns on Facebook is extremely simple. First, you want to go to your page and tap the "Promote" button. Then, Facebook will pop up with a little page asking you what your goal is for your advertisement. You can then choose from the list of options that includes: "Increase traffic to my website from Facebook," "Increase attendance at my event," "Generate new leads," "Increase the reach of our content on Facebook," or "Boost engagement on our Facebook page." Once you have chosen, Facebook will set out the parameters to begin setting up your ad.

Next, you want to begin thinking about who your target audience is. Tap "target audience – custom" and begin inputting their demographic. Facebook allows you to include everything from age and gender, to their location and interests. Use these features to identify your target audience for Facebook as this will support you in ensuring that you reach the exact audience you are looking for. As you are in putting the demographics, you will see a small "meter" at the bottom with a yellow, green, and red section. You want to keep the rating in the green section, as this ensures that you have not made your audience too restricted or too broad. Keeping your audience large and healthy, but not so large that you waste your money never being seen, is important.

Then, you want to look over your ad. You will see a small example of what the advertisement looks like. You can change the image, words, and links or buttons on the advertisement if you desire. Make sure it looks attractive. Furthermore, ensure there are little to no words in your images. Facebook avoids sharing advertisements with images covered in words, so it may reduce you getting seen.

Lastly, if you have your page linked to an Instagram business account, you can choose to cross-promote your promotion so that it reaches both Facebook and Instagram users. This is great for when you are driving traffic to your website. If you do this, make sure to toggle over to the "Instagram view" so you can ensure your ad looks great there, too. Then, set your budget and hit "promote." Facebook will then go over your advertisement to make sure that it meets their standards and criteria. Once approved, you will receive a message stating that your add is live.

Inviting Friends and Family

A simple yet effective way of getting some of your earliest followers is inviting your friends and family members to like your page. When you begin your page, you can send out a massive invite that invites everyone you have added to Facebook to support your page. This gives everyone the opportunity to show their support and lets everyone in your circle know what you are up to. This can be a great way to get your first followers and increase your engagement. Friends and family tend to be some of our most active and supportive followers, which means, they are more likely to help support and boost your engagement and increase your reach. They may also share you with their own circle, which supports you in expanding right from the start. Do not overlook this simple yet highly effective measure. It can be a great way to start out and get those earliest followers which can sometimes be a challenge to create. Once you have a few followers to start, expanding on that and getting more is easy.

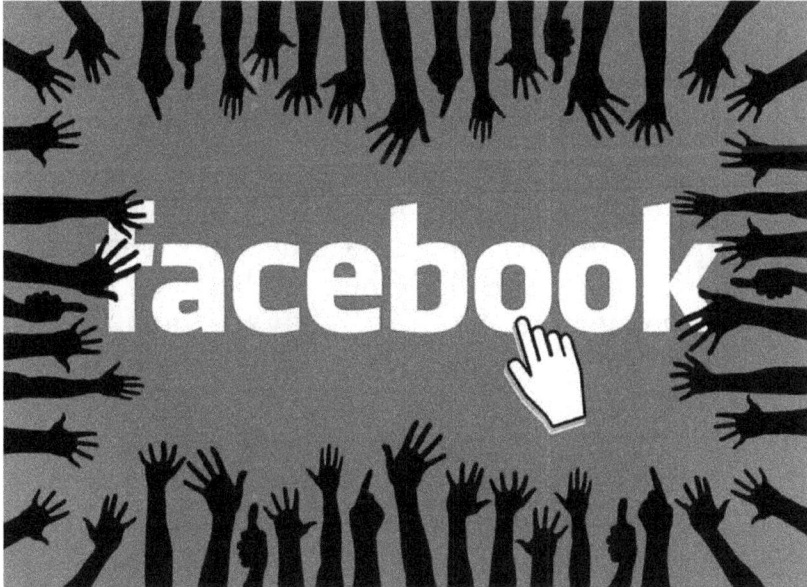

Chapter 6: Posting to Your Page

The entire purpose of using a social sharing site, beyond directly interacting with others, is posting! For that reason, you need to know how to post in order to be able to get the most out of your Facebook page. When it comes to posting, there are certain practices that work best to ensure that your posts get the biggest reach. Unlike other platforms that use hashtags or other similar measures to connect your audience to your posts, Facebook relies exclusively on algorithms that measure whether it relates and the popularity of your posts. The more popular your posts are, the more relatable they are believed to be, and therefore, the more people will actually see them.

In this chapter, we are going to explore everything you need to know about posting to your Facebook page. Make sure to follow these tips as they will support you in getting maximum engagement on your page and, therefore, getting better sales results from your following. It is important to recognize that just because someone follows your page does not guarantee that they are seeing your posts. Using these strategies will ensure that they do, maximizing your profitability.

How Often to Post

Posting on Facebook requires some consistency to stay relevant and seen. Pages that do not post regularly will not be seen as often, not only because they are not posting but because Facebook will identify them as irrelevant. The minimum amount that you should be posting every single day is at least 3 times. However, a recent study done in 2018 showed that some of the brands with the highest engagement are posting an average of 8 times per day. That being said, you are not required to maintain that level of posting. As long as you are posting three times per day, you will be keeping your page active and maximizing your reach.

There have been multiple studies done that recognize when the best times to post are. While some people prefer not to pay attention to this and simply post at rationed times throughout the day, these studies should be considered. Knowing when your audience is likely to be most active is the best way to ensure that you are seen. Studies have shown that weekday afternoons and weekends before 7 pm tend to be the most popular times for people checking Facebook. Posting at least once during these hours will help maximize your visibility and increase your engagement on your page.

What You Need to Be Posting

It is important that the content you are posting to your Facebook page is relevant and will actually attract followers. Knowing exactly what you need to be posting on your page will ensure that you are keeping a feed that is attractive and interesting to your following. This makes it so that your existing following is nourished, but also so that new followers who scroll your page will see that it is relatable and enjoyable and are more likely to follow you.

When it comes to Facebook, there are four types of posts you need to be using: entertainment, promotion, quotes, and shared. Below is a more detailed description of what each is and when you should be using it.

Entertainment Posts

Entertainment posts are any posts that are interesting or humorous to look at. Using entertainment posts as the bulk of your posts is important because it gives people something enjoyable to pay attention to. People do not turn to Facebook as an opportunity to be pitched sales to all day long. Instead, they want to find some enjoyable content that they can relate to or gain value from.

Entertainment posts on Facebook can be anything from relatable pictures to a story you share. You can post links to articles you have enjoyed that you think your audience might also enjoy. It is important to make sure that everything you post is relevant to your niche. Posting anything "just because" could result in your following not understanding what you are about and unfollowing you or not following you, to begin with.

Your entertainment posts should make up around 40% of your overall posts. This keeps your page humorous, enjoyable, and relevant.

Promotional Posts

Promotional posts are any post in which you are seeking to sell products to your audience. There are two types of promotional posts: hard pitch posts and soft pitch posts. Hard pitches are very clearly all about sales. They are the posts that include an image of a promotion you have going on or a product you want to sell with a link directly to the checkout page. When your audience sees them, they know you are selling something. These posts should have a very clear call to action, encouraging your audience to purchase the product or browse the sale. They should only account for about 5% of your total posts.

Soft pitches are pitches that have been blended with entertainment. They generally involve storytelling to some degree followed by a sales pitch. For example, say you sold a product that was meant to make traveling easier. You could tell a story about how in the past you did not have this product, so it was a challenge, but now that you have it, your most recent trip was a breeze. Then, you could conclude the post with something like "If you feel like you could benefit from something like this, check it out!", and then post a link to the product. Creating sales posts like this are more personable and tend to get your audience paying attention and interested in what you are talking about. This makes them more likely to engage with your post *and* click through to learn more about the product. These should account for about 15% of your total posts.

Quote Posts

Quote posts are posts that have been made with pictures that have quotes on them. These posts are extremely popular on social media and often result in a lot of shares. You can download and use the quote photos from other people, but it is better to make your own. Most photographs made by others are also branded for them, so this can lead to you promoting someone else instead of your own company. Occasionally, this is okay, but for the most part, your quote photographs should be made by yourself. That way you can brand it for your own company. To do this, simply put your social media handle (username) or logo on the image. Alternatively, you can put both on for more exposure. The best place to make your quote pictures is either on Canva or Word Swagg. Both are great applications that will give you the opportunity to make incredible images.

Quotes can be made by yourself, but you can also find them online. If you're borrowing other quotes, be sure to attribute the quote to who initially wrote it. This ensures that you are not imposing on any copyright laws which, as you know, are important. Also, it looks more professional to attribute the quote to the person responsible for saying or writing it. Quote posts should make up approximately 30% of what you post.

Shared Posts

Sharing posts from other pages is another great way to add content to your own page. This also makes your page more likely to get viewers. A great way to do this is to share posts from pages or businesses that are in the same niche as yours or that appeal to the same audience. Now that you know who your audience is with great clarity, you can easily recognize content that they would love to share. The best way to do this easily is to follow the same pages your audience follows and then simply share anything that seems relevant. The best shares are of viral images or videos, as these are trending and relevant and will help keep your page highly visible to your audience.

When to Boost Your Post

"Boosting a post" is a form of paid promotion offered by Facebook. Essentially, you can take a post that performed well and pays for it to perform even better. You can also boost promotional posts, as this helps expand your reach and assists you in getting more out of your sales pitches.

Depending on what your budget is for your page, boosting your posts may or may not be something you are interested in. If you are, you should know when the best time to boost your post is. Essentially, pay attention to the traction your desired post gets. If it seems to reach more people than your average post, then it may be a good idea to boost it. Often, Facebook will send you a notification letting you know when this has happened. Then, simply go through the process of promoting it. You can easily choose your target audience and then promote it to them for just a few dollars. Facebook's paid promotions require you to pay a minimum of $1/day, so promoting with their application is extremely customizable and affordable. Simply choose your budget, set your parameters, and boost your post!

How to Share Across Multiple Platforms

One great thing about social media is that you can take advantage of multiple platforms with a single post. The easiest way to do this is to actually go through Instagram. With Instagram, you can easily share your posts on Facebook, Twitter, and Tumblr. If you want to take advantage of this easy sharing feature, you will need an

Instagram profile. If you do not already have one, you might consider downloading my other marketing book: "Instagram Marketing." This will go into detail on how you can use Instagram to reach your following as well. When you cross-promote this way, you allow one post to get you much further. Rather than having to create individual posts for every single platform, you can share one post across all. This saves time and ensures that your great content maximizes its reach and its rate of return.

Marketing through Posts

Marketing through your posts on Facebook primarily relies on storytelling and relatability. In modern Facebook marketing, telling stories that people can relate to is important. Facebook is a sharing site that thrives on images *and* text, and a lot of people who are interested will want to read the text. The trick is: you only have about three seconds to capture the attention of your audience with your first words. You can easily do this by using a catchy first line that summarizes what you will find in the story. For example, "Why booze and starfish don't mix." Or "That time I lost my phone at an elephant resort." These titles should accurately reflect what the person is about to read, but should also be catchy enough that they actually want to read it.

As you tell the story, be sure to keep it fairly sweet and simple. Despite Facebook being a site where people are willing to consume more text, there is still an attention span that you need to recognize. Keeping your posts as something that can be read in thirty seconds or less is important. So, share your story effectively but in a way that is intriguing. A great way to keep people reading longer is to break your post up into paragraphs. Create a paragraph every 2-3 sentences. This breaks it up and makes it easier for your audience to read. You should also include emojis, as these help you portray the mood of the story and increase the relatability of your post.

It may take some time to master the art of marketing through storytelling, but once you do, you will realize that it is both fun and easy. This is an art of marketing that is growing more and more trendy, so be sure to take advantage of it and get on board as soon as possible.

Automating Your Page

Taking care of a Facebook page may sound needy and daunting at this point. Rest assured, however, it is not. There are many ways that you can reduce the amount of time you need to be on your page, including through automation. Automation can be done using a third party application such as Hootsuite or PostApp, or it can be done through your Facebook page itself. Which platform you use will depend on what you are looking for. If you want to automate multiple social media networks at once, using a third-party app is the way to go. If you are only automating your Facebook page, doing it directly through the page works well.

Automating your page is as simple as pre-creating posts and scheduling them to post at preset times. Ideally, you should create at least 3 posts per day to be shared in advance. Then, if you personally share any post on any given day, it simply adds to the number of posts you have shared that day. Automating your page can be done in as little as thirty minutes and can give you enough posts to last you for anywhere from a few days to a few weeks. Some will even automate their posts, including all of their upcoming promotions, for months in advance. While the initial work of having to create the posts takes some time, having your posts already created is extremely helpful.

The one thing you should be cautious of when automating posts is refraining from automating anything that is trending too far out in the future. You never know when trends will fade, or new ones will come, and you do not want to be caught sharing a trend that is no longer relevant. This will decrease your engagement and stunt a great deal of work you've put in on your page.

Chapter 7: Selling Your Product/Service Via Facebook

Once you have your Facebook page up and running, it's time to start generating your audience into customers! Remember don't hesitate to sell your service or products. You don't want to just consistently provide free value and knowledge without any return for yourself because at the end of the day you run a business. So now it's time to think of your plan of attack towards how you can sell your products and services within your business.

How to Get Started

If you don't already have a website set up, you can still promote your business just via Facebook. Posting photos, videos and Stories of your business in action or the products you sell is a good way to get your customers to trust you and want to buy. At the end of the day if they have liked your page they have an interest in what you offer and you will convert more customers than you think as long as your provide quality value that is authentic.

Driving Facebook Traffic to your Business.

If you have a product or service make sure the link to your website or the products are in your Facebook Bio as well as all your other social media accounts.

Using Stories

Stories are a great feature that was recently built in to Facebook pages, as well as private pages. This feature allows you to share exclusive, behind the scenes footage of your business in action. It gives you a great advantage in getting customers excited about what you are offering, as well as allowing them to feel personally involved in what you are doing in your business. When people support your business, they want to feel important to you and your business. Brand experience is a great way to boost that. Through stories, you can share important moments that customers would otherwise miss. This can include fun things such as unboxing new products, sharing a live video during a customer session (with customer consent,) or even just sharing a short video of what you and your staff are doing on your days off. One great thing about Facebook stories is that you can actually add to them from Instagram. If you have a business Instagram account linked to your Facebook page, when you share stories to your Instagram account you can set them to share to Facebook as well. This means that a broader audience sees your stories and that you are nurturing both platforms at the same time.

Photographs and Videos

Using posts with photographs and videos is a great way to share your business with your audience. When it comes to selling specifically, you want to make sure that you are sharing high quality images or videos of your products and services. For example, taking a high-resolution image of your product with a beautiful background in a well-lit area is a great way to make the image more attractive, thus attracting the audience to you even more. Alternatively, sharing an image of you performing a service (with customers consent) is another great way. For example, if you are a hairdresser, you might have a co-worker take a high quality picture of you cutting a client's hair. Then, you can share it with a caption such as, "Had so much fun cutting (customer's name)'s hair today! PS, I have a few more appointments available this weekend. Call xxx-xxx-xxxx to book!" This is a great way to show off your business through your posts and drive traffic to your business.

As you can see, selling through Facebook Is actually quite simple. You can get your customers to click on a specific link where you're selling your service or you can drive the traffic from your social media account to your website where you can then provide more value and sell them your products and services.

If not you can simply tell your customers via private message if they're interested in the product or service you're willing to sell.

Remember by this point you would have done your customer research and your page will be up and running providing immense value. So don't hesitate to sell your quality products.

Chapter 8: Affiliate Marketing with Facebook

If you are new to the world of business and are looking for a great way to make money with your page, affiliate marketing may be something for you to look into. Affiliate marketing is a wonderful way to make passive income on your Facebook page simply by implementing the tools that you have learned throughout the rest of this book. In this chapter, you are going to learn how you can begin affiliate marketing so that you can make money through your Facebook page without having to sell your own products or services. You can solely rely on making income through Affiliate Marketing or you can use it as an extra income stream.

Understanding Affiliate Marketing

Affiliate marketing is a business model wherein the affiliate marketer (you) markets products for other businesses. This business model is one of the lowest maintenance models to exist, allowing you to build a passive income simply through having an engaged social media following. To make money using this business model, all you have to do is share products to your followers that are owned by other brands. Every time they purchase a product with your link or coupon code, you earn a commission from the company.

Creating a powerful affiliate marketing business requires you to build an engaged and loyal following on social media first. If you do not have an engaged and active following, people will not click on your link, and you simply won't make any money. As a result, it will be harder for you to get deals. This will not be a successful venture for you.

However, if you take the time to build a loyal following through the regular posting advice given in this book, you will be able to make plenty of money through this business model in relatively minimal timing.

Alternatives to affiliate marketing include direct sales and network marketing. In direct sales and network marketing, however, you are bound to a single company. In affiliate marketing, you can have as many deals with as many companies as you desire. You create termed contracts with these companies that enable you to promote their products in exchange for a commission unlike in direct sales or network marketing where you become an official representative of the chosen company. That being said, affiliate marketing is a lot freer and more lucrative than direct sales or network marketing which is why I recommend it.

Finding Affiliate Marketing Deals

Getting started in affiliate marketing requires you to find deals that you can market. When you are a bigger online personality with a large number of engaged following, companies will begin to seek you out to do these deals. This is because they recognize the value of your marketing abilities and they want to take advantage of your services and access your audience through a person they trust most: you. When you get to this point, making your deals is pretty simple. However, until you are there, you need to know how to find affiliate marketing deals that will allow you to go through with them when your number of followers is smaller.

Once you have a few hundred followers, you can begin looking on websites like ClickBank or Amazon associates to receive affiliate marketing deals. These websites are based on connecting companies with marketers so that affiliate marketing deals can be made. Companies on these websites are looking for people just like you to promote them. All you have to do to get started is to create a profile, have it verified, and then begin connecting with companies who are ready to make deals with you.

When you are making your deal, make sure that you pay attention to the terms of it. You do not want to enter a deal that may be restrictive, limiting, or unfair to you. Some companies may want to make deals that do not involve cash. For example, they may give you product credit to their company in exchange for your services. This is not necessarily a bad thing, but you need to decide if it is something you are willing to accept. Knowing what you are and are not willing to accept into your deals will make it easier to finalize them, or negotiate them if need be.

Lastly, do not be too hard on yourself if you have a deal that is not exactly what you expected or if things started off somewhat slow. Staying dedicated and continuing to put the effort will pay off in the end. Your commitment is your success, so keep showing up. Before you know it, you will be earning a major passive income through your affiliate marketing deals.

Another way to find affiliate marketing deals is emailing the company and letting them know that you would be happy to sell their product through an affiliate program. They will give you a special link in which lets the company know that they are your customers who are buying their product/service. Some company's have an affiliate program you can automatically sign up to on their website also.

Posting Your Affiliate Marketing Posts

When you are posting your affiliate marketing posts, make sure that you verify the terms of your agreement with the company you are promoting for. Additionally, verify the terms of the agreement with the site you are sharing it on, and any legal requirements you may have. For example, recently, a law was passed stating that if you are using affiliate links in a blog post, you must post a disclaimer at the top of your post to let people know that you are being paid for promoting the company with your link.

Keeping yourself protected by knowing what is expected of you is the best way to ensure that a good deal does not go sour accidentally. If you want to remain professional, stay in business, keep your accounts active, and avoid potential lawsuits, staying protected by doing what is legally required of you is essential.

Aside from paying attention to your legal obligations, posting for your promotional posts with affiliate links is simple. Follow the information you learned about sharing promotional posts in *"Chapter 5: Posting to Your Page,"* subsection *"Promotional Posts."* These pointers will still apply as they are the best tools that you can use to promote on Facebook. If you are permitted to by the company, you may also consider boosting the post to increase visibility and maximize the amount of money you make through that link. Always be sure to ask first, however, as not all companies will be okay with you promoting their links through paid advertising.

Remember if you're going to sell an affiliate product make sure it relates to your business and it is something that you truly believe will benefit your customers. Quality and personal benefit are the main factors you want to consider when selling any type of product. And losing your customers trust can highly effect your business. Remember you are a quality provider only!

Chapter 9: Linking all Social Media Accounts

Taking Advantage of All Social media Platforms

It is highly beneficial to use other platforms such as; Instagram, YouTube, twitter, LinkedIn, Pinterest etc. If you can link all platforms together you can generate more traffic and followers to your Facebook page.

Advertising the Social Media Platforms you provide content on

On your Facebook Bio and 'About' section. Add that your username is the same for your other social media accounts.

Advertising through doing give-away's is also a good idea. You can make a post offering a free product or service, captioning: Tag 5 friends and follow all of our social media platforms for the chance to win this product or service. This works great especially if what you are giving away holds epic value.

In your Facebook cover photo, you can have all the social media logos and your username next to them so customers are reminded to follow you on their other accounts.

Another great way is to link your Instagram account to your Facebook and Twitter account. This allows you to share between the two accounts directly through Instagram. This feature works for both posts and stories. Not only will this drive people back and forth between your Instagram and Facebook accounts, but it will also give you further reach from a single post which means less time you need to spend posting.

Lastly, on your website and any other page that permits, add a Facebook icon. This will indicate that you are findable on Facebook. On your website, you can also add your link to this icon so that those who find your website can easily toggle over to your Facebook page and begin following you.

Conclusion

Congratulations on reading *"Facebook Marketing!"*

This book was designed to help you optimize your Facebook marketing experience, whether you are just getting started or you have been doing it for some time. Facebook marketing tools are incredible and in-depth tools that allow you to access your niche like never before. With incredibly accurate metrics, Facebook can narrow in on your exact target client and put you directly in front of them. For that reason, you need to know exactly who your target client is on Facebook and how you can identify them with Facebook metrics.

I hope that this book was able to support you in getting started and expanding your knowledge on Facebook marketing. From helping you optimize your page to showing you how to post so that you get more organic and paid engagement, everything has been included to support your continued success.

The next step is to stay committed and continue posting to your Facebook page on a regular basis. Keeping your page active with a minimum of three posts a day, spending time engaging with your audience and staying on-brand is the best way to boost your engagement and increase your reach. Before you know it, your page will be growing exponentially, and you will have the capacity to maximize your income through it.

Know that beginning your Facebook marketing journey may be slow at first. Because you are not yet known in the Facebook community, it may take a little bit of time before people begin to see your posts and like your page.

Trust in the process, follow the steps in this book, and do not get discouraged. Once you begin getting more *likers*, it will snowball. Your page will be growing massively in no time at all.

Lastly, if you enjoyed the book *"Facebook Marketing,"* please take the time to rate and review it on Amazon Kindle. Your positive feedback would be appreciated.

Thank you and best of luck!